T0358075

LEICHHARDT
The Great Explorer

R.T. Watts

18

KNOWLEDGE
BOOKS AND SOFTWARE

Teacher Notes:

Ludwig Leichhardt was one of Australia's great explorers. His most successful exploration was to Port Essington near Darwin from just outside of Brisbane, a journey of nearly 5,000km. His disappearance created interest for many years after his death and this mystery is still being talked about today. This is an ideal discussion starter for students as they consider the factors involved in his disappearance and speculate on what happened to Leichhardt and his team as they bravely set out to explore Australia's vast inland.

Discussion points for consideration:

1. How many expeditions did Leichhardt make and where did he go? What do you think happened on his last trip?

2. What attributes would be important for Leichhardt and his team members in order to be successful, eg leadership, goal-setting, determination, resilience, bravery, preparation skills. What else?

3. Make a list of the supplies and people you would take to trek across Australia? Why is preparation so crucial to your success?

Sight words, difficult to decode words, and infrequent words to be introduced and practised before reading this book:

Leichhardt, Queensland, Northern Territory, Kimberley, Australia, Port Essington, Western Australia, explorer, discovers, difficult, Wiradjuri, guarded, inventions, technology, university, geology, biology, medicine, sciences, excellent, collections, dangerous, Brisbane, government, Kakadu, exploration, expedition, equipment, malaria, disappeared, compass, sextant, position, direction, Indigenous, Aboriginal.

Acknowledgement of the First Nations' People: We acknowledge the Traditional Owners of country throughout Australia and recognise their continuing connection to land, waters and culture. We pay our respects to their Elders past, present and emerging.

Contents

1. What is an Explorer?

Explorers are people who travel far to find new places. An explorer must return home alive to be successful. If they die before they get back home, no one will know what they found.

Explorers went to all parts of the world. Australia was first explored by sea. Explorers sailed around Australia. It was very hard to go overland. There were no roads that they could follow. Some of the tracks they followed were made by First Nations people.

These First Nations paths would guide the explorer through the difficult parts of cliffs and gullies.

Australia was explored in stages. The first explorers headed west of Sydney. They explored the pathways going over the Blue Mountains.

Blaxland, Wentworth and Lawson explored the mountains to find a pathway to the grasslands. This was the lands of the Wiradjuri Nation.

People soon followed with cattle and sheep. This caused the loss of hunting lands for the Wiradjuri peoples and the first war started with First Nations people.

First Nations people have cared for their country for a long time. It was their country and they protected it. For 60,000 years, the land was kept for their nation. Any people wanting to come on to their country had to get permission. This was for other First Nations people and the new people.

First Nations people were now in a war with the new people. The new people came on to their land. They had sheep and cattle. These animals ate their grass and got rid of their food. Kangaroos moved as their food was no longer on these grasslands.

Wars were starting everywhere as the First Nations people fought back to try and protect their lands.

Nothing changes without explorers. Today there are explorers looking into space and the deep seas. There are other explorers looking at how far science can take our inventions.

Science, computers, energy forms and tech are the new areas to be explored. Explorers in these areas are looking into things like micro worlds or new forms of magnets to make or transfer energy. The world is facing big problems and we need people to take a chance and explore the unknown.

Australia needed to have explorers to be a great nation. Ludwig Leichhardt was a great explorer, and this is his story.

2. About Ludwig Leichhardt

Ludwig Leichhardt was born in Germany. He was a very smart student and went to university. He studied geology, biology, medicine and other sciences.

Leichhardt started travelling early and went to England. He then studied further across Europe.

His work and writings were very good. People thought that his writings and details were excellent. He was getting noticed for his work.

3. Australian Visit

Ludwig Leichhardt would have heard the buzz about Australia in England. He got the idea to travel to Australia.

Leichhardt came to Sydney in 1842. He wanted to explore and start putting together collections of plants and animals.

As well as this, he wanted to study First Nations languages, map the country, and write about how the country was farmed.

These were all big jobs. Leichhardt could have spent all his time on just one of these jobs.

Leichhardt became well known for his work in Australia. People were impressed with his writings.

He wrote about the First Nations people and he quickly made a great name for himself as an explorer.

The work that Leichhardt did was good, but he wanted to do more. He wanted to explore inland Australia.

4. First Expedition

Leichhardt's first expedition was very dangerous. He was going to leave from Moreton Bay (Brisbane) and travel to Port Essington (north east of Darwin). This was a journey of nearly 5,000 kilometres.

He would travel up over the mountains and then on to the plains. Leichhardt would then head north through central Queensland and up into the Northern Territory towards the top of Australia.

Water was always short as it was dry country. The chance of getting lost was high too.

Leichhardt's Exploration

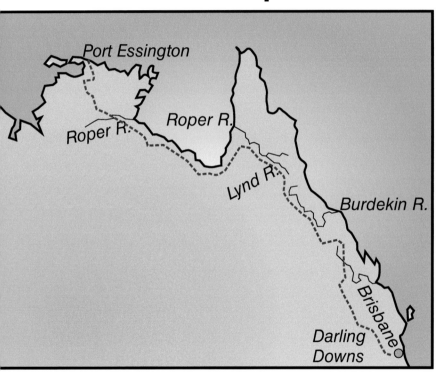

The government was going to pay for the trip, but this fell through. Leichhardt paid for the trip himself. He set off with some horses and his mates. Leichhardt did not have a lot of money.

First Nations people met him on his way through Central Queensland. They were kind to him, and told him the way north.

Seven months later he got to where Kakadu National Park is today. He was travelling north to Port Essington. It was an amazing trip to survive the heat, the attacks by First Nations people, poor food, snakes and spiders, and always being short of water.

Leichhardt then came back to Sydney by boat. He was in very poor health. The exploration had been very hard. One of the explorers had been killed in an attack by First Nations people. Most people thought Leichhardt had died as he was late and there had been no word.

Leichhardt had kept notes and maps on where he went and how he got there. He was the first person to make such a big journey.

It had taken nearly 11 months for this journey to Port Essington. He returned to Sydney and was treated as a hero.

Leichhardt became a star of explorers! He had made loads of notes and drawings. Everyone in Sydney wanted to meet this superstar explorer! This was the man to invite to parties and events.

Leichhardt went from party to party. He was very popular now. However, the people he talked to had no idea about what Australia was really like. They had just made Sydney like another England. Leichhardt had seen Australia's heart and he missed it. He was keen to go back to the real Australia.

5. Second Expedition

As the star of explorers, it was easy to get money to start another expedition. Everyone was keen to help Leichhardt this time.

In December 1846, he was off on his second expedition. He had the equipment, food and people to make it a big trip.

This expedition would cross Australia. He would leave Brisbane and go inland, and then head across Australia.

He was going to go all the way to the Swan River, Perth.

This time it was very unusual weather. The inland was normally very dry, but a lot of rain had just fallen. They had gone about 800 kilometres, but it was too hard. They had malaria from mozzies, poor food and swampy walking. They turned back towards Brisbane where Leichhardt rested to get over the malaria.

6. Third Expedition

Leichhardt studied maps and, in 1848, left again from inland of Brisbane. He took two First Nations guides and four people from a farm to help. Leichhardt was never seen again, and people had no idea what happened.

This was a mystery that was never solved. What happened to Leichhardt? He just disappeared. He was very good at bush survival, so what happened? Let us look at this mystery.

7. The Search for Leichhardt

Many people have tried to find Leichhardt. They have tried many times to find out what happened to him and where he died.

The trip was going to take 2 to 3 years, so people did not expect him to make contact straight away. It was not until 1851, after he was gone for 3 years, that people got worried.

In 1852, the NSW Government put together a search party. This search party did not find Leichhardt, but they did find a clue. They found a campsite with an "L" letter over "XVA". This could mean "L" = Leichhardt and the "XVA" could have been a Roman numeral.

The Roman number "XVA" is likely to be a date. Scan the QR code below and try and work out the possible date. It does not make sense, so the "A" could have been another number. Try and figure out this puzzle. Leichhardt left tree marks on all his trips. This tree mark on the following page, was on his first expedition to Port Essington.

The "L" mark was also found in other trees. Searches were made to find marks or pieces of things that may have been Leichhardt's.

It is common for explorers to mark their direction. This is like a "way mark" on a GPS system today. In those days it was by compass and sextant. This is the same way that sailors found their position, direction and speed on the ocean.

The explorer could get their position and speed over the ground by looking at the stars and the position of the sun.

Twenty years after he went missing, people were still looking for Leichhardt. There were stories of bones and horses killed by First Nations people.

There were sightings of remains that people thought were those of Leichhardt. The stories were strong enough for the WA Government to send an expedition. This expedition to search for Leichhardt was led by John Forrest.

Forrest found nothing except some campsites which they thought were used by Leichhardt.

The mystery of Leichhardt disappearing was always a story people talked about. People and newspapers would make up stories about his disappearance.

The governments were interested in doing what the people wanted. This meant more stories about Leichhardt and the mystery of his disappearance.

There were more than 14 expeditions sent over the years to try and find out what happened.

A reward of over £1000 pounds was offered to help find Leichhardt. This would be worth about $150,000 today. This was a lot of money! It was offered by a newspaper.

More clues kept being found. A cattle bone was found. This was believed to be a clue because cattle were not normally found in this area. Leichhardt had travelled with some cattle.

Aboriginal people spoke of a group of white men drowning, dying of thirst, and starving.

Cooking pots were found along with forks and knives. Camp fire equipment was also found. Tent pegs were found and pieces of iron. All these clues suggest that Leichhardt probably got to Western Australia.

Nearly 50 years after Leichhardt had disappeared there were more traces of clues. The explorer David Carnegie met some Indigenous people in the deserts of Central Australia.

The First Nations people showed Carnegie something very interesting. It was a tin lid from a matchbox. The iron piece was from a saddle. They said it was from a group of white men who came through a long time ago.

They said that there had been four white men and two aboriginal guides who died of thirst.

Leichhardt made it close to the Gibson Desert. Why? There was evidence found, and stories told in that area.

Indigenous rock paintings show part of this story. It shows men with rifles. These rifles are above their heads. These paintings were in Kakadu which is a long way north of where Leichhardt was supposed to be.

The man has a broad hat, riding a horse and holding a rifle. This is an explorer. Was it Leichhardt on his desert crossing or from his prior trip to Port Essington?

A new clue is a small brass plate. This had "Ludwig Leichhardt 1848" on a piece of wood which was part of a burnt rifle. Tests were done on this brass plate and found it was made of metal from 1800. It also had gunpowder from the correct time period. This piece was not a fake.

The remains were found in an old boab tree which was in the desert of Western Australia. This is interesting as it matches what Leichhardt was trying to do. He was trying to go around the deserts to the north, closer to the Kimberley coast.

You be the judge!

a/ Where did Leichhardt die?

Western Australia?

Queensland?

Northern Territory?

b/ Why did he die?

Attacked by Indigenous people?

Lack of water?

Lost and died of hunger?

The mystery is a great Australian puzzle which has never been answered. Leichhardt helped us learn more about Australia and its inland areas. He was a super star explorer!

Word Bank

Leichhardt	paintings
Queensland	interesting
Northern Territory	starving
Kimberley	equipment
Australia	probably
Port Essington	newspaper
Western Australia	disappearing
explorer	sextant
mystery	malaria
Indigenous	kilometres
pieces	expedition